An Oak Tree

Tim Crouch

methuen | drama
LONDON • NEW YORK • OXFORD • NEW DELHI • SYDNEY

METHUEN DRAMA
Bloomsbury Publishing Plc
50 Bedford Square, London, WC1B 3DP, UK
1385 Broadway, New York, NY 10018, USA
29 Earlsfort Terrace, Dublin 2, Ireland

BLOOMSBURY, METHUEN DRAMA and the Methuen
Drama logo are trademarks of Bloomsbury Publishing Plc

First published in Great Britain by Oberon Books 2005

Tenth anniversary edition published 2015

This edition published by Methuen Drama 2023

A catalogue record for this book is available from the British Library.

A catalog record for this book is available from the Library of Congress.

ISBN: PB: 978-1-3504-3760-9
ePDF: 978-1-3504-3762-3
eBook: 978-1-3504-3761-6

Series: Modern Plays

Typeset by Mark Heslington Ltd, Scarborough, North Yorkshire

To find out more about our authors and books visit
www.bloomsbury.com and sign up for our newsletters.

AN OAK TREE

An Oak Tree previewed at the Nationaltheater Mannheim, Germany, on 29 April 2005, and premiered at the Traverse Theatre, Edinburgh, on 5 August 2005.

Co-directed by Karl James and Andy Smith
Original sound design by Peter Gill
Piano played by Simon Crane
Originally produced by News From Nowhere with Lisa Wolfe
www.timcrouchtheatre.co.uk

Tim Crouch's *An Oak Tree* was remounted in 2023 by Francesca Moody Productions, touring to Bristol University (as part of the drama department's 75th anniversary), Festival d'Avignon and the Royal Lyceum Theatre at the Edinburgh Festival Fringe.

Written by Tim Crouch
Directed by Tim Crouch, Karl James and Andy Smith
Music by Peter Gill
Piano played by Simon Crane

Performed by Tim Crouch and a different second actor at every performance

Produced by Francesca Moody Productions
   Executive Producer – Francesca Moody
   Associate Producer – Grace Dickson
   Production Assistant – Elly Roberts

Tim Crouch

Tim Crouch is an Obie-award winning writer and theatre-maker based in Brighton, UK. His plays include *My Arm*, *An Oak Tree*, *ENGLAND (a play for galleries)*, *The Author*, *I, Malvolio*, *Adler & Gibb*, *Beginners*, *Total Immediate Collective Imminent Terrestrial Salvation*, *Superglue*, *Truth's a Dog Must to Kennel* and (with Andy Smith) *what happens to the hope at the end of the evening*. Directing credits include *House Mother Normal* (New Perspectives/Brighton Festival); *I, Cinna (the poet)*, *The Taming of the Shrew* and *King Lear* (RSC); *PEAT (*Ark, Dublin); *Jeramee, Hartleby and Ooooglemore* and *Beginners* (Unicorn Theatre) and *The Complete Deaths* (Spymonkey). *Beginners* won the 2019 Writers Guild of Great Britain Best Play for Young Audiences. Tim created and co-wrote *Don't Forget the Driver*, a six-part series for BBC2 which won Best TV Comedy at the Venice TV awards, 2019.

timcrouchtheatre.co.uk

@thistimcrouch

Karl James

Karl has co-directed Tim Crouch's *My Arm*, *An Oak Tree*, *ENGLAND*, *The Author*, *What Happens To Hope At The End of The Evening*, *Adler & Gibb* and *Total Immediate Collective Imminent Terrestrial Salvation*.

Most of Karl's time is spent as director of *The Dialogue Project*, enabling people to have conversations when the stakes are high. His audio work has featured on BBC's radio series Short Cuts, in *A Different Kind of Justice* for BBC Radio 4, at Latitude Festival and in Third Coast's Filmless Festival in Chicago. Karl's podcast series is called *2+2=5* and his book on how to have better conversations, *Say It and Solve It*, was published in 2013.

thedialogueproject.com

understandingdifference.blogspot.com

Andy Smith

Andy Smith is a theatre-maker who has collaborated closely with Tim Crouch since 2004, most recently co-directing (along with Karl James) *Truth's A Dog Must to Kennel* (2022) and *total immediate collective imminent terrestrial salvation* (2019). Other recent works include *COMMONISM* (2018, in collaboration with Amund Sjølie Sveen), *SUMMIT* (2018) and *The Preston Bill* (2015). He is currently developing *CITIZENS' ASSEMBLY*, one of a series of plays designed for groups of people to meet, read together, and then discuss. He is a part-time lecturer in theatre practice at the University of Manchester.

andysmiththeatre.com

Francesca Moody Productions

Francesca Moody Productions

Francesca Moody Productions commissions, develops and presents brave, entertaining and compelling new theatre. They work with the UK's leading playwrights and discover and nurture new talent to produce bold, award-winning shows with universal appeal and commercial potential.

Since launching in 2018 the company has been awarded an Olivier and four Scotsman Fringe Firsts, been nominated for a Tony Award, and produced work in London, New York, on tour across the UK and at the Edinburgh Festival.

Current and upcoming productions include: *A Doll's House* (Hudson Theatre, New York); *School Girls; Or, The African Mean Girls Play* (Lyric Hammersmith); *An Oak Tree* (Festival d'Avignon, Royal Lyceum Theatre Edinburgh); *Kathy and Stella Solve a Murder* (Underbelly Edinburgh, Bristol Old Vic, HOME Manchester) and *Feeling Afraid as if Something Terrible Is Going to Happen* (Bush Theatre).

Recent productions include: *A Streetcar Named Desire* (Phoenix Theatre); *Lemons Lemons Lemons Lemons Lemons* (Harold Pinter Theatre); *Berlusconi: A New Musical* (Southwark Playhouse Elephant); *Kathy and Stella Solve a Murder* (Roundabout); *Feeling Afraid as if Something Terrible Is Going to Happen* (Roundabout); *Mum* (Soho Theatre); *Leopards* (Rose Theatre) and *Baby Reindeer* (Bush Theatre, Roundabout).

FMP are also the creators of Shedinburgh Fringe Festival an online live-streamed festival of theatre, comedy and music created in lieu of the Edinburgh Fringe in 2020. Since its launch the festival has raised over £40,000 towards a fund to support the next generation of artists to make it to the Fringe.

FMP is led by Francesca Moody MBE, who is best known as the original producer of the multi-award-winning *Fleabag* by Phoebe Waller-Bridge, which she has produced globally on behalf of DryWrite, most recently at the Wyndhams Theatre, when it was also recorded and broadcast by NT Live, playing in cinemas throughout the world. In 2020 Francesca led and coordinated the Fleabag for Charity campaign and later the Theatre Community Fund with Phoebe Waller-Bridge and Olivia Colman, raising over £2 million to support theatrical artists and professionals whose livelihoods and creative futures have been threatened in the wake of Covid-19.

francescamoody.com

@FMP_Theatre

INTRODUCTION

This book is a gallery.

Tim Crouch once described words as 'the ultimate conceptual art form'. Words are strange things; they that can exist in an uncountable number of different forms, fonts, sizes, media; they can be spoken or sung or signed or written or printed or imagined; a handful of letters on a page can make you think, make you unreasonably happy, make you cry, and more; they can be invented anew, they can change their meanings, and they can peacefully die away; they can be chiseled into a gravestone and they can be impossible to get out of your head; they can describe the world and they can change the world. They point at concepts but are also conceptual things in themselves; like fairies in *Peter Pan*, they only exist because we believe in them.

And if the word is a conceptual art form, then this book – which is full of them (go on, flick forward, it's true!) – is a sort of gallery of conceptual art.

There's a tricky question buried in that description of words, which is about the relationship between words and the world. Words don't resemble the world they seem to describe. The word 'theatre' doesn't look or sound like a theatre. Even onomatopoeic words don't sound all that much like the things they represent. So how do we come to represent the world through them?

This philosophical question is a practical question for the theatre. What is the relationship between a play on the page and a play in the theatre? Does the text define how the play must be done? If so, in what way and to what extent? If a playwright writes 'The FATHER nods his head', some parts of the stage picture are being defined, but others not. We don't know what the FATHER looks like, his height, how old he is, the colour of his hair, whether he has a beard, what he's wearing, his expression, and much more. We know that he nods his head, but not how: quickly? slowly? thoughtfully? eagerly? Is it a big vigorous motion or an almost imperceptible gesture? And just because the FATHER nods, does the *actor* have to? There are many ways of informing an audience that this has happened: someone could read the stage direction out; the gesture could be projected on a screen; it could be inferred from the way the HYPNOTIST reacts; or, if you like, the actor playing the FATHER could nod his head.

Sometimes, the theatre seems to forget that it has these choices to make. In some parts of our theatre, it will seem as if the actor nodding his or her head is the 'obvious' or 'natural' or 'correct' or 'simplest' or 'clearest' or 'most real' way to represent this direction. Since the late nineteenth century, British theatre has been in thrall to the view that the theatre should represent the world by trying to resemble it as closely as possible. This was not always the case; it would be a mistake to think that audiences at the theatre of Dionysus or at Shakespeare's Globe sat there frustrated that they weren't looking at more realistic scenery. In those theatres, it would seem, there was a clearer understanding that the theatre functions imaginatively: we are taken into a fictional world and whether that world is represented through realistic sets or random objects or words or sounds that evoke the imagination, these are still conceptual choices we have made.

An artist that Tim Crouch likes to refer to is Marcel Duchamp, one of the first artists to place concepts at the centre of his work, who made an important distinction between retinal art and conceptual art. Retinal art is grasped mainly through the eyes (on the retina); conceptual art is grasped with the mind. In fact, even in the most literal and realistic theatre show, there are always things that only exist for us conceptually; the past and future of the characters, the world offstage, the psychological states of people we are looking at. Most realistic theatre isn't all that realistic either: actors generally talk much louder than the characters would, walk about in rooms much larger than the characters would; to some extent we just choose to see them as realistic.

Tim Crouch puts the conceptual rather than retinal aspects of theatre front and centre but, in doing so, he reminds us that all theatre is like this. When, in *My Arm* (2003), he tells the strange story of the play using random objects gathered from the audience, we might well reflect that this is always the case; it's to some extent arbitrary whether we represent a battle on stage by using onstage actors or offstage sounds or the words of a narrator or a short abstract physical sequence. When in *ENGLAND* (2007), he has the main character of the play represented simultaneously by two people, we might well reflect that all casting is to some extent arbitrary, that if we can accept young people playing old people or men playing women or poor actors playing Kings or, in the case of James Bond, several different people playing the same person, why should we insist that on stage one character must be played by one actor?

This might make *An Oak Tree* sound very abstract and airless. But it's the opposite. What Tim Crouch and his collaborators understand is that the conceptual nature of theatre underpins all theatre from *Antigone* to *Les Misérables*, from *Waiting for Godot* to *Run For Your Wife*. You can't have fun or be moved or be filled with joy without partaking in the theatre's conceptual playfulness.

Several apparently unusual theatrical devices structure the experience of *An Oak Tree*: first, in a beautifully childlike way, all of the theatre's transformational power happens in front of us:

Hypnotist   Ask me what I'm being, say: 'what are you being?'

Father   What are you being?

Hypnotist   I'm being a hypnotist.

This fundamental part of theatre, the transformation of one thing into another thing, one person into another person, is part of what we might call the magic of theatre. But here the magic is spoiled. Or is it? Do we ever really believe in the transformations in front of us? Indeed, the more captivating the transformation that an actor achieves, aren't we more admiringly aware of the actor? When a movie actor undergoes a massive transformation – make-up, latex reshaping the face, a fat-suit to change the body shape – we always delight in reading the details of the very process that was apparently supposed to erase the actor's persona.

It might seem as if seeing behind the mask would rob the mask of its effects, but the opposite turns out to be true. Maybe after all we don't actually ever believe really, like the audience at a bad (or even good) hypnotism act, we pretend to believe in the illusion because we know that, like the fairies in *Peter Pan*, like words, the theatre only exists if we believe in it.

In *An Oak Tree*, there is a scene where an actor plays a hypnotist playing a mother, another actor plays a father repeating lines given to him right in front of us, a chair plays a baby and a piano stool plays an oak tree – and, despite all that obvious fakery, it is one of the most moving scenes I've seen in a theatre this century.

The second major device is that the second actor is new to every performance. They don't know the play, don't know the part, don't know the lines. They're told carefully what they have to do, but they literally don't know where they're going. It's an unusual experiment, but it's also not unprecedented. Parts in a play are called 'parts' because, in the Elizabethan period, when it cost a lot of money to have a play copied out, actors would just be given their own lines and cues and find out about the whole play only in rehearsal or performance. (Or, to pick a more contemporary and eccentric example, the actor Tom Baker – best known as the fourth Doctor Who – famously didn't read the scenes he wasn't in, claiming that to do so would 'feel like prying'.) The effect of this in performance, apart from emphasising the way in which the transformation really is happening in front of us, is to intensify the precarious liveness of the performance. With the actor being given bits of paper to read from, instructions over the headset, lines to repeat, instructions to carry out, our consciousness of the possibility of failure is enormously enhanced.

The precariousness of the device fills *An Oak Tree* with vulnerability and tenderness. The theatre's provisionality and precarity, its liveness and risk are sharpened and deepened by the second actor, giving new intensity to the dreadful delicacy of the Father's grief and the Hypnotist's regret. The actor is the audience's avatar, knowing little more than we do about the course of the play, and in performance I think you can feel the whole audience willing the second actor on, expressing a kind of care for that second figure, as character and actor and person. It also intensifies our sense of ourselves as an audience, gives us a peculiarly intense sense that we're all, actors and spectators, in the room together making this all happen. It gives us a fleeting sense of our very connectedness as people, and allows us to glimpse that our mutual responsibilities, our overlapping imaginative landscapes, our care for one another are precious things that don't just happen, that – like fairies in *Peter Pan*, like words, like theatre – our humanity only exists if we believe in it.

Caryl Churchill described *An Oak Tree* as 'a play about theatre, a magic trick, a laugh and a vivid experience of grief, and it spoils you for a while for other plays'. It does sort of spoil some other theatre for a while, because it acknowledges what other theatre often seeks to ignore. The joy of *An Oak Tree* is that it explains away how all theatre works, but then does it anyway.

Dan Rebellato

THANKS

To all the second actors, past and future.

The Peggy Ramsay Foundation. Mark Ravenhill, Paines Plough and Hannah Ringham. Thomas Kraus and the Nationaltheater Mannheim. The David Knight Hypnotic Experience. The Nightingale Theatre, Brighton. Philip Howard, Orla O'Loughlin and the Traverse Theatre. Lisa Goldman and Soho Theatre. Ros Ward and the BBC World Service. James Hogan, Charles Glanville, Andrew Walby and Oberon Books. Martin Platt and David Elliot and the Perry Street Theatre. Dan Fishbach, Michelle Spears, Will Adashak and the Odyssey Theater, Los Angeles. David Greig, David Dey and the Royal Lyceum Theatre, Edinburgh. Chris Dorley-Brown. Michael Craig-Martin. John Retallack. Tim McInnerny. Simon Crane. Lisa Wolfe. Jonny Reed and Oats, Catherine Hargreaves. Tiago Rodrigues. Magda Bizarro. University of Bristol Drama Department. Francesca Moody. Grace Dickson. Julia, Nel, Owen and Joe. Andy Smith and Karl James for doing brilliantly.

And to the memory of Roger Lloyd-Pack, Jon Beedell, Marcello Magni and Jenny Harris, head of education, National Theatre, 1990–2007.

SECOND ACTORS IN TIM CROUCH'S PRODUCTION OF *AN OAK TREE*
(at time of publication, July 2023)

Rehearsal 2005: Ian Golding, Cath Dyson, Hannah Ringham.

German previews 2005: Alex Miller, Tom Hartmann.

UK previews 2005: Deborah Asante, Emma Kilbey, Dan Ford, Alister O'Loughlin, Jo Dagless, Anna Howitt, Matthew Scott, Natalie Childs.

Edinburgh Festival Premiere 2005: Rebecca Thorn, Claire Knight, Sandy Grierson, Ant Hampton, Tom Brooke, Annie Ryan, Sarah Belcher, Al Nedjari, Paul Blair, Hilary O'Shaughnessy, Brian Ferguson, Stevie Ritchie, Matthew Zadjac, Gabriela Murray, Ciaran Bermingham, Mark Ravenhill, Waneta Storms, Andrew Clark, Tom Espiner, Jon Spooner, Ross Manson, Jason Thorpe.

Ireland 2005: Barry McGovern, Deirdre Roycroft, Dennis Conway, Martin Murphy.

UK touring 2006: Amelda Brown, Johnny O'Hanlon, Richard Talbot, Nick Walker, Nic Jeune, Pooja Kumar, Richard Croxford, Maria Connolly, Miche Doherty, Kathy Keira Clark, Tristan Sturrock, Mary Woodvine, Emma Rice, Kevin Johnson, Chris Bianchi, Toby Jones, Helen Kane, Hayley Carmichael, Toby Park, James Wilby, Christine Molloy, Christopher Eccleston, Gin Hammond, Roger Lloyd Pack.

Lithuania 2006: Sakalas Uzdavinys.

Latvia 2006: Ivars Puga.

Israel 2006: Marcello Magni, Kathryn Hunter.

Russia 2006: Roman Indyk, Alexander Vartanov, Maria Popova.

Portugal 2006: Beatriz Batarda, Cathy Naden, Andre e Teodosio, Joao Pedro Vaz.

Finland 2006: Taisto Oksanen, Auvo Vihro.

Italy 2006: Lella Costa, Elio de Capitani, Laura Curino.

US previews 2006: Richard Kamins, Angela Reed, Carmela Marner, Gene Marner, David Bridel, Peter Gaitens, Camilla Enders, Johana Arnold, Ed Vassallo.

Barrow Street Theatre, New York 2006/7: Peter Van Wagner, Rachel Fowler, Lucas Caleb Rooney, Michael Cullen, Mark Blankenship, F. Murray Abraham, Charles Busch, Reed Birney, Randy Harrison, James Urbaniak, Kristin Sieh, Leslie Hendrix, Steve Blanchard, Laurie Anderson, Amy Landecker, John Shuman, Jeremy Bieler, Kelly Calabrese, Michael Countryman, Laila Robbins, Pearl Sun, Joan Allen, Maja Wampuszyc, Christopher Cook, Maura Tierney, Alison Fraser, Frances McDormand, Mary Bacon, Tamara Tunie, Ray Dooley, Brooke Smith, John Judd, Richard Kind, Matthew Arkin, Craig Wroe, Michael Cerveris, Marin Ireland, Peter Dinklage, Alysia Reiner, Tim Blake Nelson, Chuck Cooper, Ben Walker, Austin Pendleton, Alix Elias, Mark Consuelos, David Pasquesi, Mike Myers, David Rasche, Chris Eigeman, Lili Taylor, Kathleen Chalfant, Joey Slotnick, Bob Balaban, Adam Rapp, Mary Testa, Hunter Foster, David Hyde Pierce, Stephen Lang, Kathryn Grody, Scott Foley, Jay O. Sanders, Alan Cox, Denis O Hare, Alan Ruck, Lisa Emery, Frank Wood, Mark Saturno, Nicole Orth-Pallavicini, Erik Jensen, David Mogentale, Alexandra Neil, Brian Logan, Katie Finneran, Walter Bobbie, Wendy Vanden Heuval, Tovah Feldshuh, Carolyn McCormick, Maryann Plunkett, George Demas, Christopher Durang, Judith Ivey, Jim Dale.

Canada 2007: Patrick MacEachern, Kelly Dawson, Joel Smith, Heather Kolesar, Maiko Bae Yamamoto, Kathryn Shaw, Marcus Youssef, Jonathan Young, John Krich, Erin Ormond, Trevor Hinton.

Soho Theatre 2007: Paterson Joseph, Sophie Okonedo, Ruth Sheen, Tracy-Ann Oberman, David Morrissey, Ed Woodall, Phelim McDermott, Amanda Lawrence, Anna Francolini, David Harewood, John Ramm, Selina Cadell, Anthony Vendetti, Tracey Childs, Jeremy Killick, Gina McKee, Juliet Aubrey, Michael Simkins, Saskia Reeves, Celia Meiras, Tricia Kelly, Hugh Bonneville, Paul Hunter, Adrian Scarborough, Linda Bassett, Eve Best, Kwame Kwei Armah, Gary Winters, Janet McTeer.

UK tour 2007/2008: Richard Headon, Sam Troughton, Josie Lawrence, Richard Katz, Ben Keaton, Jonathan Keeble, Brigit Forsyth, Claudia Elmhirst, Bill Champion, Louise Dearden, Mark Calvert, Terry O'Connor, Deka Walmsley, Jon Whittle, Nathan Rimell, Cora Bissett, Julie Brown, Murray Wason, Siwan Morris, Richard Elis, Ged Stephenson, Vic Llewellyn.

Brazil 2007: Rodrigo Nogueira, Guilherme Leme.

BBC World Service 2007: Tim McInnerny.

Singapore 2008: Loong Seng Onn, Jean Ng, Karen Tan, Ivan Heng.

Quebec 2008: Kevin McCoy, Robert Bellefeuille, Anne-Marie Cadieux.

Melbourne 2008: Jane Turner, Geoffrey Rush, Julia Zemiro, Kim Gyngell.

Hong Kong 2009: Lynn Yau, Jonathan Douglas, Fredric Mao.

Brown University, USA 2009: Matt Clevy.

Odyssey Theatre, Los Angeles 2010: Meagan English, Peter Gallagher, Clancy Brown, Lisa Wolpe, John Rubinstein, Kurtwood Smith, Jesse Burch, Dan O'Connor, Jennifer Leigh Warren, Beth Grant, Joe Orrach, Peter Van Norden, Stu Levin, Jason Alexander, Peter Macon, Stacie Chaiken, Christopher Michael Moore, Michelle Monaghan, Anne De Salvo, Miguel Sandoval, Lauryn Cantu, Alanis Morissette, Alexandra Billings, Kathleen Early, Carolyn Seymour, Floyd Van Buskirk, Kyle Secor, Alan Cumming, Rich Sommer, Michael Gladis, Megan Gallagher, Alex Kingston, Wendie Malick, Josh Radnor.

UMASS, Amherst, USA 2010: Marcus Gardley, Milan Dragicevich, Julie Nelson.

Bios, Athens, Greece, 2011: Yota Argyropoulou, Yannis Sarakatsanis.

Bangkok, Thailand, 2012: Pattarasuda Bua Anuman Rajadhon, Nophand Boonyai.

Dublin 2012: Nyree Yergainharsian.

Rehearsals 2015: Gerard Bell, Peter Hobday, Hannah Cooper-Dean, Amy Griffiths.

National Theatre 2015: Conor Lovett, Maggie Service, Kate Duchêne, Philip Quast, Stephen Dillane, Naomi Wirthner, Samuel Barnett, Kiruna Stamell, Nicholas Karimi, Sharon D Clarke, Penny Layden, Nick Holder, Ashley McGuire, Trystan Gravelle, Chook Sibtain, Pearce Quigley, Richard Henders, Jodie McNee, Patrick Marber, Sarah Cameron, John Heffernan, Samuel West.

Traverse Theatre 2015: Ewen Bremner, Jamie Michie, Aoife Duffin, Sharon Duncan-Brewster, Caitríona Ní Mhurchú, Gary McNair, Lucy Ellinson, Ned Dennehy, Simon McBurney.

Bristol Old Vic 2015: Neve McIntosh, Akiya Henry, Fionn Gill, Simon Shepherd, Kate O'Flynn, Jon Beedell.

Warwick Arts Centre 2015: Luke Barnes, Lou Platt, Charlie Josephine.

RADA 2018: Susan Wokoma.

Orange Tree, London 2018: Kate Hardie.

Central School of Speech and Drama, London 2018: Shelby Bond, Claudia Heinrichs.

Teatro Sarmiento, Argentina 2018: Ingrid Pelicori, Luciano Suardi.

Bristol University Wickham Theatre 2023: Pippa Haywood, Adele James, Polly Frame.

Avignon Festival 2023: Natacha Koutchoumov, David Geselson, Teresa Coutinho, Cynthia Loemij, Adama Diop.

NOTES FOR A PROSPECTIVE SECOND ACTOR FROM Tim Crouch

This is a document I send to any prospective second actor. For me, it is important that they read it before agreeing to do the show with me.

What is *An Oak Tree*?

It's a play with two actors. I'm one of them. The second actor, ideally, will have neither seen nor read the play before they walk on stage with me at the start. I can't enforce this but I know that the experience is stronger for everyone if that's the case. If you're interested in doing the show, **please** don't read it or watch clips of it on YouTube. This is a chance to let go of something and respond to the moment. *An Oak Tree* is only the moment.

As the second actor in performance, you would never be asked to generate words of your own. Everything you say in the play (and everything I say in the play) is scripted. I say the play IS improvised; it's just not improvised with words. Your performance (with words) would be given to you through a variety of devices: by direct and very simple instructions, by me speaking to you through an earpiece, by reading from pieces of script. I guide the second actor throughout the performance openly and carefully. I pay attention and work to ensure you have space and that you feel supported, enabled and successful. Everything the second actor needs is given to them – by the time they need it. Not before.

There is no right way to do *An Oak Tree*; there is no wrong way. There is the way it's done each performance and it's different every time – even though every word of it is scripted. The invitation the play makes to both actors – me and you – is to be open.

This device of the second actor intricately supports the story the play tells.

What's needed?

An Oak Tree is around 70 minutes in performance. The total time commitment needed is a little over two hours. More if you'll let me get you a drink afterwards.

At times, the second actor will sight read from text that I give to them in performance. These are scenes in the play – carefully laid out on the page, in font no smaller than size 14. The second actor will also wear wired earphones for some of the show. If you're comfortable with sight-reading and happy to wear earphones, then you're good to go.

I would meet you in the theatre an hour before the show. In this time no information is given that is indispensable – nothing you need to remember. The hour is useful to get a feel for things, for us to get to know each other a little and to address any questions that exist. We test levels on a microphone and practice with a separate bit of script to get a sense of our voices in the space. There is no preparation needed prior to this, no costume, no rehearsal, nothing.

A caution: the story of *An Oak Tree* concerns the loss of a child. The play also mentions ideas of suicide. I'd be very happy to talk to you if this raises any concerns. Please get in touch.

PREPARING FOR A PERFORMANCE OF *AN OAK TREE*

I meet the second actor in the empty theatre an hour before the play begins. I let them know that nothing in that hour is essential; that the play will be given to them moment by moment in performance; that on a need to know basis everything they need to know will be given to them *by the time they need to know it*; that all the work in rehearsal has been about them and their journey through the play. The hour before is like a private first act of *An Oak Tree* – an act without an audience. I talk about the requests the play makes of us both: an invitation to be open to what happens and not to predetermine how they're going to be; an invitation to listen, to play, to tell a story. I talk about the 'given circumstances'; some of which are the fiction of the story and some of which are the reality of what's happening i.e. that they're in a play they don't know. My invitation to them is to play the given circumstances! I talk about how the play will switch back and forth and I invite them not to get 'locked' in any one state. I talk about the fluidity of any idea of character in the play – that they will be both themselves and not themselves and that the audience will do the work of differentiating between the two. That they'll only come unstuck if they decide to demark an idea of character with an accent or a voice or a particular physicality. I advise them against doing this! I say that they will learn a lot from how I model the journey alongside them. I invite them again to be open and to play with me.

I tell them that they can't get it wrong. And that they can't get it right. There is no 'right way'. Just the way we'll do it that evening, which will be different to how it's ever been or how it ever will be because it's us this one time only. I say how this is an easy thing for me to say, but a harder thing for them to accept. I say that the play will always wait for them; that the 'boat' will never leave without them; that we can stop and start and go back and anything is allowed. I say how the play is actually strengthened by the cracks in it. I say how the audience will be on their side because they're one of them; they're discovering the play at the same time as the audience.

I talk a bit about how words will be given to them during the performance. About how a speech will be fed to them through an earpiece they will wear at times. We put the earpiece in and we practice with how it feels with me giving them instructions and things to say. They practice with the microphone which they will use one time in the play. (I don't want them to be phased by any technical aspects – they have enough on their plate being open to a play they don't know.) And I talk about how they'll be given script and how the invitation of the script is to play as any actor might in a workshop situation – to 'get it on its feet' and to dive in. We then practise with a piece of text that has been written specially to practise with. It gives them a sense of how the text will be laid out, how spaces between lines denote possible space in performance, which 'character' they will be reading in the play (me reading HYPNOTIST and them reading FATHER) and a sense of their voice in the space. We play the text in the two ways it will be delivered in performance: once as direct address to the audience with both of us reading out. And again as a 'scene' with me off-book. Below is the practise text we use which also gives them a hint at the idea of the story.

This all usually takes about 45 minutes. After which I hand the second actor a ticket for the play and I show them the reserved seat in the audience I'd like them to be in at the start. They're then welcome to hang out with me or go find their friends, etc. We then hand the space to the front of house staff and that's it. When I get clearance I walk on stage and the play begins.

PRACTICE TEXT

(To be shared and read with the second actor in the meeting before the show.)

Hypnotist To begin with, can you tell me what happens in this play?

Father Yes, of course.

Pause.

I change a tree into my daughter.

Hypnotist Okay.

Does the tree become a symbol of your daughter?

Father No. It's not a symbol.

I change a tree into my daughter.

Hypnotist But surely it's not your daughter. It's a tree.

Father Yes. It's a tree.

But it's also my daughter.

Hypnotist Can you prove it?

Father Well, yes and no.

I claim that my daughter has become a tree and, as you will see, she has.

Hypnotist But you haven't simply called this tree your daughter?

Father Absolutely not.

It's not a tree anymore.

I would be surprised if anyone told me they saw a tree.

Hypnotist I see.

And how long will it continue to be your daughter?

Pause.

Father Until we change it.

A NOTE FROM Andy Smith

Introduction

Hello. In your hand you are holding a play called *An Oak Tree*. It's by Tim Crouch. You are about to see it, or read it. Perhaps you have just watched it, or perhaps you saw it some time ago. Whichever it is, thanks for coming, or for showing an interest in the book and picking it up and taking a look. Welcome.

You can often find a bit of writing like this published with the text of a play. Sometimes it is referred to as the programme note. Its intention is to perhaps provide you the reader or audience member with some pearl of wisdom: supply a key that unlocks just a little of what you are about to see/read/have just seen/have just read/might just read/might buy/might put back on the bookshelf of the shop/other (delete where applicable). It might be that the note gives you the reader or audience member an outline of the story. Or maybe it gives some background information about the rehearsal processes, or the themes and form of the piece. It might even make reference to a significant incident in the life of the writer that has moved them to write it, or write in general. It may give you some ideas about what they wanted to say with this particular play. You may have realised by now that this may not be one of those programme notes. Of course, having not finished it, I don't know either.

Information

I'm really glad I got the job of writing it, though. When I go and see plays and performances I always love reading these things. The anticipation! I sit there, waiting for the play to begin, attempting to absorb quickly all the stuff that I have mentioned. And sometimes afterwards I re-read the programme, and think about it in relation to what I have seen. It's so great to get an opportunity to write one!

You will have noticed, though, that I am having a bit of trouble with it. My problem is that I don't want to be presumptuous or complicated, and I don't want to reveal too much. I'm also getting distracted thinking about the other interesting information that is in this book too. Perhaps on the page before or after this there's a list of characters, or some biographies of the people who worked on the play. There's probably a list of thanks, those pages are so great to read too! If there's only a minute to go before the play begins, please don't think it would offend me if you want to look at those first. If you do, I'll just say thanks for reading this bit to here, and I hope you enjoy *An Oak Tree*.

Perhaps you've stuck with me (cheers!) or come back to carry on reading this afterwards (welcome back! What was the performance like tonight? Good, I hope). Perhaps you are reading the play now, some years after it happened. I am thinking about you too, standing there in a bookshop or library reading this introduction, trying to get an idea about what it's about and maybe even thinking about buying (or borrowing) it. Go on! You might have a great time, if reading plays is your thing.

No lines

I am aware that you may be very dissatisfied with this programme note. 'It's not really telling me anything,' you might be thinking (or even remarking to your neighbour). I think it's a great privilege to be able to go and see plays and read about them in the programme note, but I just don't want to get into writing any of that problematic stuff about what the work means, does, or why it exists. I think that you are probably able to work that out by yourselves. So I am going to take this opportunity to tell you a story I have just remembered.

During a conversation about *An Oak Tree* in Germany,[1] Tim Crouch said something about what he might have been thinking about when he was writing it. He said (and I am very aware that I may be paraphrasing him) that he wanted to think about a critical situation where he, or a character, might feel like they are performing in a play without a text, in scenes where they did not know the lines. At the time this seemed like an important thing, and it feels that for the purposes of this programme note it could be interesting to share it with you. I certainly think that it relates to the story that you are about to read/see (has the performance still not begun? what are they doing?). It also, I think, relates very strongly to the way the story is told.

You see, when we make and watch and talk about theatre we can have all sorts of conversations about the phenomena of it: about the live qualities of theatre, how it happens right in front of you, how we can move through space and time in different ways. We can talk about the reality of the theatre, about the truth of it, and how as well as being very real and here and now there might not be anything real at all here. For example, in this particular play you'll find a line I really like which talks about how you have all gone home, but you're actually still there!

---

[1] I don't know if it is important that you know we were in Germany, but it certainly sounds impressive. Also, I love footnotes. They always seem to lend an importance to a piece of writing, even when they don't particularly say anything!

It's fascinating. Oh no! I said I didn't want to get into the problematic stuff!

But seeing as we have, before I go, what I would like to say is this: what I really hope is that plenty of these thoughts and conversations (and more) can be found in this play called *An Oak Tree*, and also that we can and should have them. Even more, though, I just want to say that I hope that you enjoy seeing or reading it. Thanks.

Andy Smith, August 2005

EXCERPTS FROM…

an oak tree
1973
objects, water, and text
Collection: National Gallery Of Australia
By Michael Craig-Martin

(There is a glass of water on a shelf. This is an oak tree, a work made by Irish-born artist Michael Craig-Martin in 1973. Beside the glass of water there is a text:)

Excerpt 1

Q. To begin with, could you describe this work?

A. Yes, of course. What I've done is change a glass of water into a full-grown oak tree without altering the accidents of the glass of water.

Q. The accidents?

A. Yes. The colour, feel, weight, size…

Q. Do you mean that the glass of water is a symbol of an oak tree?

A. No. It's not a symbol. I've changed the physical substance of the glass of water into that of an oak tree.

Q. It looks like a glass of water.

A. Of course it does. I didn't change its appearance. But it's not a glass of water, it's an oak tree.

Excerpt 2

Q. Do you consider that changing the glass of water into an oak tree constitutes an art work?

A. Yes.

Q. What precisely is the art work? The glass of water?

A. There is no glass of water anymore.

Q. The process of change?

A. There is no process involved in the change.

Q. The oak tree?

A. Yes. The oak tree.

Q. But the oak tree only exists in the mind.

A. No. The actual oak tree is physically present but in the form of the glass of water.

(Reproduced by kind permission of Michael Craig-Martin)

An Oak Tree

For Pam and Colin

'The distinction between fact and fiction is a late acquisition of rational thought – unknown to the unconscious, and largely ignored by the emotions.'

Arthur Koestler

Note

Eight chairs, stacked at the sides of the stage. One piano stool in the middle of the stage.

One hand held wireless microphone. Bold print indicates amplified speech through the microphone.

An onstage sound system and speakers.

Hypnotist. Father.

Hypnotist in a costume – silver waistcoat, etc. **Father** in whatever everyday clothes the actor chooses to wear.

The actor playing the **Father** (the second actor) can be of any gender and of any adult age. They will be completely unrehearsed in their role, and will walk on stage at the beginning with no knowledge of the play they are about to be in.

At times, the second actor will wear wired headphones connected to a wireless receiver – this enables the **Hypnotist** to speak to the second actor through a microphone without the audience being able to hear. This script contains examples of instructions to be given by the **Hypnotist** to the second actor. They are given as guidelines, but detailed attention must be given to these instructions to ensure a constant feeling of support and success for the second actor.

Sections of script are prepared on clip boards. At times, the second actor (and sometimes the **Hypnotist**) will read from these scripts.

The Bach referred to in this script is the Aria from the Goldberg Variations. It is a flawed rendition, as if played by a child: faltering but ambitious, failing to resolve until the very end of the play when it moves into the First Variation.

Prologue

*The actor playing the **Father** is sitting in the audience. The **Hypnotist** walks on stage.*

Hypnotist   Ladies and gentlemen. Good evening/ afternoon. My name is (*the name of the actor playing the **Hypnotist***). Welcome to (*the name of the venue*).

Would you come up and stand here, please?

*The **Hypnotist** invites the second actor out of their seat in the audience and onto the stage.*

Ladies and gentlemen. This is X. (*The name of the second actor.*) X will be performing in the play this evening/afternoon. X has neither seen nor read it.

X and I met up about an hour ago. I have given them a number of suggestions. I've suggested that they enjoy themselves!

But the story is as new to X as it is to you.

Scene One

*The **Hypnotist** hands the second actor a page of script: 'Could we just read this together, you and me?' The second actor reads the part of the **Father** from the script.*

Hypnotist   Hello!

Father   Hello!

Hypnotist   Thanks for this.

Father   It's a pleasure!

Hypnotist   You hope!

Father   Yes!

Pause.

Hypnotist   How are you feeling?

Father   Okay.

Hypnotist   Nervous?

Father   A little.

Hypnotist   It'll be fine. You'll be fine.

Father   I'm sure.

Hypnotist   Any questions before we start?

Father   Not really.

Hypnotist   Nothing?

Father   How long is the show?

Hypnotist   It's just over an hour.

Father   Okay.

Hypnotist   Anything else?

Father   I don't know if I'm allowed to ask this . . .

Hypnotist   Go on.

Father   How *free* am I?

Hypnotist   Every word we speak is scripted but
otherwise . . .

Father   Okay.

Hypnotist   Anything else?

Father   Not really.

Hypnotist   Just say if you feel awkward or confused and
we'll stop.

Father   Okay.

*The **Hypnotist** takes the **Father**'s script from them.*

Hypnotist	Great!
	Can I ask you just to look at me.
	Ask me what I'm being. Say, 'What are you being?'
Father	What are you being?
Hypnotist	I'm being a hypnotist.
	Look.
	I'm fifty-nine years old. I've got a bald head, a red face and bony shoulders. (*This must be an accurate description of the actor playing the* **Hypnotist**.)
	Look.
	I'm wearing these clothes. Look.
	Now ask who you are, say 'And me?'
Father	And me?
Hypnotist	You're a father. Your name's Andy. You're 46 years old, you're six foot two. Your lips are cracked and your fingernails are dirty. You're wearing a crumpled Gore-Tex jacket. Your trousers are muddy, your shoes are muddy. You have tremors. You're unshaven. Your hair is greying. You have a bloodshot eye.
	That's great! You're doing really well!
	Also, you'll volunteer for my hypnotism act. You'll volunteer because I accidentally killed your eldest daughter with my car and you think I may have some answers to some questions you've been asking. I won't recognise you when you volunteer. I won't recognise you because, in the three months since the accident, you've changed.
	We've both changed.

Pause.

	There.
	That's about as hard as it gets, I promise.
	Let's face out front. Ask who they are, say 'And them?' (*ie. The audience.*)
Father	And them?
Hypnotist	They're upstairs in a pub near the Oxford Road. It's this time next year, say.
	Let's say they're all a bit pissed.
	But don't worry, X, they're on your side. It's me they're after.
	Face me.
	I'm just going to talk to them. I won't be a second.
	(*To the audience.*) Ladies and gentlemen. In a short time I'll be asking for volunteers from the audience but I'm not asking you. I'm asking some people in a pub a year from now. So please don't get up.
	(*To the* **Father**.) That's them dealt with!
	Are you okay? Say 'Yes'.
Father	Yes.
Hypnotist	Good. Really good.
	Let's start. You can put your headphones in, and switch on your pack.

The **Father** *puts in their earpiece and switches on the receiver.*

Hypnotist	We take our time. We're in no hurry.
	Would you go and sit back in the audience?

The **Hypnotist** *motions the* **Father** *to their seat in the audience.*

The **Father** *sits in their seat in the audience.*

Hypnotist   Good luck!

You'll be great.

The **Hypnotist** *moves upstage to the onstage sound system.*

A moment. A gathering.

Three. Two. One.

Scene Two

The **Hypnotist** *puts on music. Carmina Burana, O Fortuna. Very loud.*

Through the music, the **Hypnotist** *arranges chairs into a row across the stage, with the piano stool in the centre. He then visits the second actor (in the audience) and tells them, 'I'm going to ask for volunteers from the audience. I hope no one will volunteer! You will volunteer, but only when I talk to you in your ear-piece. Don't do anything until I talk to you in your ear-piece. Just sit back and watch the show. And thanks!'*

The **Hypnotist** *takes up his microphone.*

O Fortuna ends.

The **Hypnotist** *'enters' the stage.*

The **Hypnotist**'s *language is broken and faltering.*

Hypnotist   **Ladies and gentlemen.**

I will welcoming.

I will.

I.

Welcome you to this –

To my hypnotic world.

To my hypnotic world.

In a short minute's time I'll be looking for such certain volunteers to come with and join me here on this chairs these. These volunteers that they're –

Now, when before I ask these some hypnotic volun – superstars to come with join me, there is one are one or two things that I'd like to tell you about hypnotic about hypnosis, about stage hypnosis, about the things you're going to see tonight, ladies and gentlemen, or rather not rather not rather the things you'll never see in any of my shows.

Firstly. I will never lie to you, ladies and gentlemen. You will see no false nothing false tonight. Nothing phoney. No plants, no actors. The people you will see on stage tonight, ladies and gentlemen, apart from myself, are all genuine volunteers!

You are the stars of the stars of this evening's –

Of all my shows, ladies and gentlemen, all my shows are completely clean. Nobody will reveal any secrets tonight. In the shy, tonight, nothing nothing nobody will reveal any sexual fantasies tonight. There's no stripping in tonight's show. And there's absolutely no sex in at all it.

Sounds shit, doesn't it!

There is one are two types of peerson who cannot be voluntised – hypnotised. The first type is anyone who is mentally unstable. If you're mentally unstable please remain in your chair.

There may be some ladies here, ladies here who, ladies who are pregnant. If you are pregnant, congratulations, but please don't voluntise teer for tonight's shy. There may be some ladies who are not pregnant but would like to be. Come and see me after the show and I'll sort you out.

Now, in a few moments –

I've got about ten chairs. Nobody will reveal any secrets and nobody will take their clothes off, but apart from that anything could happen.

Come up, ladies and gentlemen, and give me a piece of your mind.

I'm going to play some music. While the music's playing, if you have an open mind, if you're a game, you're gain for a a laugh and you're over eighteen, then I'd like you to join me on this these chairs.

I'm going to stepping back.

I'm stepping back so you can come forward.

I'm going to play some music.

I'm just the hypnotist, ladies and gentlemen; you're the stars of the show.

Come up, ladies and gentlemen, and give me a piece of your mind.

Your mind.

Your mind.

Using the onstage sound system, the **Hypnotist** *switches on cheesy 'come-on-down' music.*

Music plays.

No volunteers.

If audience members do volunteer, they are gently thanked and guided back to their seats by the **Hypnotist**.

The **Hypnotist** *feeds instructions to the* **Father**'s *headphones* –

>*'When I've finished speaking to you, I'd like you to count to five in your head and then, in your own way, in your own time, come up onto the stage and sit on the piano stool facing the audience.'*

With the music still playing, the **Father** *'volunteers' for the show – walking onto the stage and sitting on the piano stool.*

The moment is held.

Music stops.

The sound of passing road traffic.

The **Hypnotist** *sits beside the* **Father**.

Hypnotist   You're by the side of a road now, not far from here.

This is the place where your child was killed. You come here regularly. The truth is you can't keep away. This is the sound of the roadside. Whenever you hear this sound, that's where you are.

It's six-thirty in the morning. You've been here for three hours. It's dark and cold and the air is damp.

You're near a street lamp and you're next to a tree.

You're on the phone. Your mobile phone. You're calling home. You want to speak to your wife. Your wife's name is Dawn. Your younger daughter picks up the phone. Her name is Marcy.

The **Hypnotist** *may feed the* **Father** *the following instruction:*

> 'Keep looking out to this road. Don't repeat anything now, X. Just listen to what you say.'
>
> You say: 'Marcy, Marcia, baby, not now.'
>
> You say, 'Tell mummy it's me, darling, would you? Would you baby?'

A lorry thunders past.

> You say, 'Dawn, love, I'm sorry. I couldn't sleep. Dawn.'
>
> You say, 'I'm weaker. I'm weaker than you.'
>
> You say, 'She's here, love. She's here. I'm with her now.'
>
> It's starts to rain. Your face flushes with colour.
>
> You say, 'Dawn. Dawn.'
>
> You say, 'Fuck you.'

The **Hypnotist** *gently offers up the microphone to the* **Father**.

Hypnotist   Would you say 'Fuck you' into this microphone.

Father   **Fuck you.**

A lorry thunders past.

Hypnotist   The phone's dead. You're cold in this rain. By this roadside. By this tree.

Dawn will come to get you. In about fifty minutes. Towards the end of the play. She'll bring Marcy. She'll tell you that it's fucking freezing. The two of you will argue. You'll argue about the nature of this piano stool. She'll say, 'It's a tree, Andy, it's just a fucking tree'.

The **Hypnotist** *goes to the onstage sound system. Roadside sound stops as the* **Hypnotist** *switches on the cheesy music again. We're back in the show.*

The **Hypnotist** *turns to an empty chair in the line of chairs.*

Hypnotist   **Have you ever been hypnotised before, young lady?**

X, come and sit on this chair and then say 'No'.

The **Hypnotist** *offers his own microphone to pick up the* **Father**'s *replies.*

Father   **No.**

Hypnotist   **Well there's a first time for everything, isn't there, ladies and gentlemen. What's your name, gorgeous?** Say 'Amanda'.

Father   **Amanda**.

Hypnotist   **That's a beautiful name for a beautiful girl. Isn't she beautiful, ladies and gentlemen? Sit back Amanda, relax and enjoy.**

What's your name mate?

The **Hypnotist** *turns to another empty chair in the line.*

Move to this chair and say 'Richard'.

Father   **Richard**.

Hypnotist   **He's a good looking lad, isn't he, girls. A bit of eye candy for the ladies! Just sit back, Richard, sit back and relax!**

And you sir, what's your name?

Move to this chair and say 'Keith'.

Father   **Keith.**

Hypnotist	**It's Keith Richards, ladies and gentlemen!** (*ie. A man called Keith and a man called Richard are sitting next to each other. A joke.*)
	You ever been hypnotised before, Keith?
	Say 'yeah'.
Father	**Yeah.**
Hypnotist	**Hey, well you'll know when what well you to do, won't you.**
	What's your name, darling?
	Sit on this chair and say 'Jacqui'.
Father	**Jacqui.**
Hypnotist	**A bit nervous, Jacqui? Or maybe just a bit pissed!**
	Nothing to be nervous about, Jacqui. Just sit back, relax and enjoy the show.
	Sit on the piano stool.
	Although, Jacqui, I tell you what, it's *him* I'd be nervous of. (*Referring to the second actor who is now on the piano stool.*)
	What's your name, mate?
	Say, 'Can I have a word?'
Father	**Can I have a word?**
Hypnotist	**Can you have a word?! Yes, mate, you can have a word! Um, 'Bollocks!' That's a word, isn't it? Got a right one here, haven't we, ladies and gentlemen, going to have to keep our eyes on that one!**
	Come sit on this chair and a big smile out.

The second actors smiles.

             I thought I said no one with a mental illness! What's your name, mate?

             Say 'Neil'.

Father   **Neil.**

The **Hypnotist** *kneels. A gag.*

Hypnotist   **What's your name, mate.**

             Say 'Neil'.

Father   **Neil.**

Hypnotist   **Your wife in, Neil?**

             Say, 'Wanker'.

Father   **Wanker.**

Hypnotist   Go and sit on the piano stool.

             Right mate. Okay!

             Thanks very much, Neil, if you'd like to go back into the audience and rejoin your party!

The **Hypnotist** *puts 'Neil's' chair over on its side and elicits a round of applause from the audience for 'Neil'.*

             Ladies and gentlemen, a round of applause for Neil!

             I want this show to be a good one. I really do. I was doing a a a gig just last week. Everything brilliant. Everyone hypnotised. Everyone doing everything I asked them to do.

             And just before the end of the show, just before the end I, er, I slipped off the edge of the stage, arse over tit. And the last thing I said before I landed was 'Fuck me'. Couldn't sit down for a month!

             A week.

*The **Hypnotist** stops the music.*

The sound of the roadside is there.

*The **Hypnotist** talks to the **Father** through headphones – inaudible to the audience.*

> *Beautiful, X. You're by the side of the road again. It's a really important place for you. It has a really strong emotional charge, this place. When I finish speaking, I'd like you to count to maybe five in your head and then, in your own way and your own time, bring your arms out in front of you, as if you were hugging a tree.*

*The **Father** brings out their arms.*

A lorry thunders past.

> *Fantastic. Just keep that position.*
>
> *I'm going to play some different music. When the music starts, I want you to very slowly lower your right arm until it's as low as it can go. And at the same time I want you to slowly, slowly, raise your left arm as high as you can. You can take about thirty seconds, a long time. Start moving your arms when the music begins. Your left arm will go up, your right arm will go down.*

*The roadside sound stops as the **Hypnotist** switches on different music – hypnotic trance music.*

Hypnotist   Now, I'm as as that weight is taking your right hand down I want to imagine that on your left hand, your left hand I'm attaching a helium filled balloon. There, I'm tying a helium filled balloon around your left left wrist and I want you to imagine that your left arm is getting lighter and lighter and starting to float up higher and higher and higher. That's great!

> Really good. Lighter and lighter. Fifty times
> higher. Fifty times lighter.
>
> (*To an empty chair.*) No weight, Ian? Nothing?
> Not even – Thank you, if you'd like to go back
> to the audience and rejoin your party.

The **Hypnotist** *puts down the empty chair ('Ian's' chair).*

> Ladies and gentlemen, a round of applause
> for Ian!

The **Father***'s arms are getting more extreme.*

Hypnotist   Close your eyes and just let yourself give
              yourself go to the to the image of the image
              that I'm giving you. And really feel the weight
              of the weight and the lightness of the
              lightness. Fifty times lighter. Fifty times
              heavier –

> All right. Great. No balloon, Jacqui?
>
> It's absolutely fine, Jacqui. Only a bit of fun.
> If you'd like to rejoin your party. Ladies and
> gentlemen, Jacqui!

The **Hypnotist** *puts down another chair ('Jacqui's' chair).*

> Keith, was it? Nothing? As we say in
> hypnotism, Keith, if it's not there it's just not
> there! Go back to the audience and rejoin
> your people. Ladies and gentlemen, Keith!

The **Hypnotist** *puts down another chair ('Keith's' chair).*

> Aren't they doing well?

The **Hypnotist** *talks to the* **Father** *through the earphones –
inaudible to the audience.*

> *The* **Hypnotist** *is going to ask you to put your arm
> down, but I don't want you to. Don't put your arm
> down until I tell you. Not long now!*

> Now I'm going to pop that balloon and I'm
> going to cut that weight, and I want all of you
> now just to bring your arms DOWN.

The **Hypnotist** *switches off the hypnotic trance music.*

> **Bring your arms down.** (*To the imaginary other
> volunteers.*) **That's great. Bring it down. Bring
> your arm down, mate.** (*To the* **Father** *who still
> has their arm up.*) **Alright, and stop. Stop it.
> Let's all just stop this, shall we? Put your arm
> down.**
>
> **He's funny, isn't he ladies and gentlemen? A
> bit of a joker.**
>
> **You think you're very funny, don't you, sir. A
> night out with your mates, have a few pints.
> Fuck around. We think it's funny, don't we?
> Don't we, ladies and gentlemen?**
>
> **What's your name, mate?**
>
> Say 'I can't move my arms'.

The **Hypnotist** *picks up the* **Father***'s replies with his microphone.*

Father	**I can't move my arms.**
Hypnotist	**Do you think I was born yesterday? Cut it out.**
	Say 'Please untie me?'
Father	**Please untie me?**
Hypnotist	**A right one here!**
	Put your arm down, mate.
	Say 'I can't move'.
Father	**I can't move.**
Hypnotist	**Stop fucking around. This bit's finished. Isn't it, Shirley? Richard?**

Take your time, look me in the eyes and say,
'Please help me'.

Father   **Please help me.**

The moment is held.

The sound of the road side again.

*The **Hypnotist** gives the following instructions directly to the
Father:*

Brilliant. You can relax your arms. You're
doing really well. Take your time. Enjoy
yourself.

I want you to count to maybe ten in your head,
and then just stand up.

*A moment by the road. The **Father** stands up.*

*The **Hypnotist** talks to the **Father** through the headphones.
Inaudible to the audience.*

*You're by the side of this road again. This is a really
important place for you. This is the place where your
daughter was killed. And you come here every
morning and you watch the cars go by. Here, where
you are now, by this road.*

*Now, in that place, in your own time and in your
own way, I want you to lie down on your back on the
floor in front of you.*

*The **Father** lies down on the floor.*

A lorry thunders past.

*As the **Hypnotist** instructs the **Father** through the headphones, he
puts down two more chairs, until there are just three remaining –
including the piano stool.*

*Brilliant. Now we're going to have some fun! For the
moment now, I want you to do exactly what the*

Hypnotist says. Just do everything the Hypnotist tells you to do.

Hypnotic trance music starts again.

The **Father** *still lying on the floor.*

Hypnotist   . . . on a golden, sandy beach.

Beautiful. Lovely. Nice and relaxed. Nice and relaxed. Aren't they relaxed, ladies and gentlemen? Feel the warmth of the sun beating down on your body and feel your body sinking in to the nice warm golden sand. That's lovely.

And now, now, I want all three of you to get up off the floor and come and sit yourselves back on your chairs on the stage. That's it. All three of you.

The **Father** *sits on the piano stool.*

Two of the other chairs remain standing.

Hypnotist   And now, these chairs aren't your normal chairs, oh no. These are special chairs. These are chairs on stage at the Albert Hall! You're on stage at the Albert Hall, you better believe it, Shirley! And I'm going to play some different music, and when the music starts all the ladies and gentlemen in the audience want to see you play the piano. Don't we ladies and gentlemen? You're going to play the piano for the ladies and gentlemen. Nod your head if you understand.

The **Father** *nods their head.*

Hypnotist   The music's going to play. When the music plays you're onstage at the Albert Hall and you're going to play . . . the . . . piano!

The **Hypnotist** *stops the trance music and starts some honky-tonk piano music.*

The **Hypnotist** *gives the following instruction to the* **Father**:

> Keep on playing. Play the piano and really get into it, enjoy it. Close your eyes if you like. Go for it. Have as much fun as you like! When the Hypnotist says 'Sleep' that's when you stop. The Hypnotist saying 'Sleep' is your only cue to stop.

The **Hypnotist** *puts down the remaining two chairs. 'Aren't you going to play for the ladies and gentlemen, Shirley?' etc. Only the* **Father** *playing the piano on the piano stool is left, surrounded by eight chairs scattered around the stage. The moment is held.*

Hypnotist   **What's he doing, ladies and gentlemen? What is he doing? Someone put you up to this? Is this a trick, is it, a joke, is it?**

You're not convincing, mate. You're not believable. We don't believe you. We can see you're trying it on, can't we, ladies and gentlemen? The show's over, isn't it, ladies and gentlemen? A piece of shit, wasn't it? Couldn't hypnotise a fly, could he? We just want to forget about it, don't we, turn back to our drinks. Don't you, ladies and gentlemen? They know this isn't a piano, you know this isn't a piano. There's no piano there. There was never a piano. You can't do this. We don't believe you. You can't – You can't. Stop it. FUCKING STOP IT.

And sleep.

The **Hypnotist** *stops the piano music. The* **Father** *stops playing.*

Hypnotist   **Bit of a wanker, here, isn't he, ladies and gentleman? Thinks he's a bit of a star, doesn't he? Friend of yours, is he? Anyone know him?**

Nobody? Shall we have a bit of fun with him, eh? See what he's really made of. Shall we? Because we all know he's only putting it on, don't we? We all know somebody's put him up to this.

Open your eyes, mate.

Listen, mate. I'm going to count down from three. And when I get to one, you'll get up, you'll look down and you'll see that you're absolutely bollock naked. Completely starkers, in front of all the ladies and gentlemen. Nod your head if you understand.

Nod your head.

And not only that, but when you hear this sound (*The* **Hypnotist** *makes a fart sound.*) you'll be convinced that you've shat yourself. That warm shit is running down the back of your naked leg. Nod your head if you understand.

And then –

And then, when I click my fingers, you'll become convinced you've done something terrible, and you'll feel really guilty – truly terrible, ladies and gentlemen. When I click my fingers, you'll be convinced convinced that you've killed someone. Yeah. You've killed a little girl, a girl, haven't you, and you'll feel really awful. Nod your head if you understand.

This should be fun, shouldn't it, ladies and gentlemen? We're looking forward to this, aren't we?

And, three, two . . .

The **Hypnotist** *gives instructions directly to the* **Father** – *audible to the audience.*

Hypnotist   The Hypnotist is going to humiliate himself far more than anyone else in this exchange now. Do what he asks you to do. Your cue to stop is 'Sleep'. 'Sleep' is your only cue to stop.

. . . One!

The **Hypnotist** *makes a ghastly, jaunty, clownish music play.*

Hey, mate, stand up. Oh, where have all your clothes gone? Eh? Ladies present, mate. Show a bit of respect. And, oh, look at your little chap. Cold out, is it, girls? Where is he, won't he come out to play? That must be a bit embarrassing. Listen to this, mate. Listen to this. (*Makes a farting noise.*) **Oh, dear, mate, what's happened there, eh? Oh dear, that's a bad smell. Couldn't you have waited? Urgh, all down your leg and all. How do you feel about that? Pretty bad, eh? Pretty apologetic towards me, I imagine. And to everyone. Stinking up the place with your stinky shit. Like you want to say sorry, I should think.**

Say 'Sorry'.

Father   Sorry.

Hypnotist   **Louder.**

Father   Sorry.

Hypnotist   **Say, 'Sorry for my stinky shit'.**

Father   Sorry for my stinky shit.

The **Hypnotist** *clicks his fingers.*

Hypnotist   **And what about that kid. A girl was it? Didn't see her coming? What were you doing? You were driving your car, weren't you? Driving**

along, were you. Drive along. Put your hands
on the wheel. Drive. Look at you, you're
driving! Turn and wave at the audience as you
drive your car along.

The **Hypnotist** *gets the* **Father** *to mime driving.*

Hypnotist   She wasn't looking, was she? Maybe she was
listening to music, silly girl! Here she is, a
little girl, here she is. And there's you in your
car. Just stepped out, didn't she. Look out,
mate, look where you're going! Look out for
that girl. Look out! Oh, and she's dead! You
killed her! Think of her little body. Think of
her poor mummy and daddy. Just driving
along, were you? How does that make you
feel? What do you wish you were? I bet you
wish you were dead! Say it. What do you
wish? You wish you were dead. Say 'I wish I
were dead'. SAY IT.

Father   I wish I were dead.

Hypnotist   Louder.

Father   I wish I were dead.

Hypnotist   What?

Father   I wish I were dead.

The **Hypnotist** *instructs the second actor.*

Hypnotist   Keep driving along, keep waving to the
audience and keep telling the audience that
you wish you were dead until I say 'Sleep'.
Keep going, even when the music stops. 'Sleep'
is your only cue to stop.

Father   I wish I were dead, etc.

Hypnotist   **All right. Enough. Stop. STOP. FUCKING
STOP THIS.**

*The **Hypnotist** stops the clownish music. The **Father** keeps driving an imaginary car and keeps saying, 'I wish I were dead'. The moment is held.*

Hypnotist   **And SLEEP.**

*The **Father** stops.*

Hypnotist   **What are you doing? What's happening? Why are you doing this to me? What are you doing here? Why are you here?**

Say 'I'm Andrew Smith'.

*The **Hypnotist** picks up the **Father**'s words with the microphone.*

Father   **I'm Andrew Smith.**

Hypnotist   Say 'I'm Claire's dad'.

Father   **I'm Claire's dad.**

Hypnotist   Say 'The girl'.

Father   **The girl.**

The Bach piano music plays and stops.

Hypnotist   Oh God. Oh Jesus.

An audible instruction is given immediately:

The piano's going to play. I'm going to go down to my knees now. Just watch me.

*The Bach plays. The **Hypnotist** collapses to his knees.*

Bach stops.

*Bach plays. During it, the **Hypnotist** sets up and instructs the **Father** for the next scene.*

*The **Hypnotist** gives the following instruction:*

Hypnotist   Great. End of Act One! We're going to read together now, you and me. I'm going to get you some script. I won't be a second.

The **Hypnotist** *gets the appropriate pieces of script.*

> We read this directly out to the audience. Take your time. Make it your own. Feel your way. We start when the music stops.

Bach keeps playing.

Bach stops.

Scene Three

*The **Hypnotist** and the **Father** stand side by side, facing out. Both read from scripts.*

Hypnotist   That evening. Dusk.

Father   That evening.

Watching Claire leave – her headphones on, sheet music stuffed into a bag. A five minute walk to the lesson.

Dusk.

Hypnotist   This was my route. A fiftieth birthday party in a sports hall. I had to phone and cancel. I said there'd been an accident, but I didn't give details.

Father   That night. That night has a colour, a touch and a sound. Dawn was back. We waited for Claire. We stood at the door for Claire. Marcy was watching *The Simpsons*.

Blue. We waited for Claire in blue. We stood at the door in red. We brushed against each other in slate grey. We looked at our watches in yellow. Dusk.

Hypnotist   I was driving a Ford Focus estate. One-point-six litres. The car was good. The brakes were good. ABS. Airbags. In the back, speakers,

sound board, microphones, costumes. My
lights were on. November.

Father   Purple. Our pulses raced in purple. We
phoned the piano teacher in brown. Our
stomachs knotted in green. The policeman
walked up the path in grey. We watched him
from the window in orange. He took off his hat
at the door in gold. White. Dawn's knees gave
way in white.

Hypnotist   This is the point on the map. This is the
Ordnance Survey grid reference. This is the
Street View. This is the bend on the road. This
is the black spot. These are the leaves by the
kerb.

Father   Death. Death walked through into the lounge.
He put his helmet on the piano stool, spoke to
us in silver. He then pronounced two concrete
blocks in black and left them to hang inside my
ribcage, pushing against my lungs. Where they
remain to this day. Recently I asked Dawn if
she thought I should go to the doctors to
arrange to have them removed. 'Where's my
man?' she screamed. 'Where's my fucking
husband gone?'

Hypnotist   These are the yellow lines, the white lines. This
is the quality of the light. This is the tree by the
verge. This is the tree. This is the view from the
North. This is the view from the South. This is
my hand, reaching down for a cigarette. For a
second. At 37, 38, 39. Twenty metres. In the
dusk. This is the girl. Stepping into the road.
Her headphones on. Some piano music. On
the way to her lesson.

Bach plays and stops.

Bach plays. The **Hypnotist** *feeds the following instructions to the* **Father**:

> Fantastic. Beautiful. Come and stand here. We're going to go back to that moment when I was on my knees, and we're going to carry on from there.
>
> I'm going to get a bit more script. I won't be a second.

The **Hypnotist** *gets the appropriate piece of script.*

> Now we work together. We act together. We start when the music stops.

Bach continues to play.

Scene Four

The **Hypnotist** *goes down on his knees – to the position he was in at the end of Scene Two.*

The Bach stops.

The **Father** *reads from their script. The* **Hypnotist** *has no script.*

Hypnotist   Look, let's get out of here. I'll buy you a drink. I had no idea you were –

Father   A drink of what? What?

Hypnotist   Look. This isn't the best –

> We should find somewhere more – Hang on. Let me talk to the audience. I won't be a second.
>
> **Ladies and gentlemen.**
>
> **I'd like to apologise for – If you'd be so kind to wait just a few moments, I'm happy to refund your tickets. In the meantime, I can**

only apologise – Please, this performance is now over. The bar is open.

Look, let me give you my – we can – I need to –

Father   I'm so sorry.

Hypnotist   No, no. It's me. I'm – As you can see, things haven't been going too well. I'm just honouring old bookings. It's not –

Father   I need to wipe this up –

Hypnotist   What?

Indicate the back of your legs and say 'This'.

Father   This.

Hypnotist   I don't understand.

Father   I'm so sorry. I don't know what happened. I need a towel or something, something to cover – In front of all these people. I don't know what happened. It's not like me.

Hypnotist   What?

Indicate the backs of your legs again and say 'This'.

Father   This.

Hypnotist   No. There's nothing. It was a suggestion. There's nothing there. You didn't –

You're fully clothed.

There's no mess there. It was me. I was doing it. I hypnotised you. I put you under.

I didn't think you'd – I thought nobody had – I thought you were taking the piss. People take the piss. I didn't recognise you. It's been three months since –

Father　　No. Look. I'm dirty. I need –

Hypnotist　No. I'm sorry.

Father　　Yes. Smell. I feel awful. This is not –

Hypnotist　Yes. Yes. Alright. I'm sorry. You're naked. You have shit down your legs.

Father　　Yes. I'm sorry.

Hypnotist　Listen. Listen.

Here. Let me clean you up. Here, with this cloth.

The **Hypnotist** *presents an imaginary cloth to the* **Father**.

Hypnotist　This is the right kind of cloth, isn't it? Say, 'Yes'.

Father　　Yes.

Hypnotist　Soon get you clean.

Stand here and face straight out.

The **Hypnotist** *wipes the back of the* **Father**'s *legs with the imaginary cloth.*

Hypnotist　There.

Father　　I'm sorry about the girl.

Hypnotist　What?

Father　　The girl I killed. What was her name?

Hypnotist　What?

Father　　The girl I killed. I was driving. You said. I'm sorry.

Hypnotist　No. No, that was – That was me. You didn't –

There was no girl.

Father　　Yes.

Hypnotist	Yes, there was, but not you. You did nothing. Me. It was me. You did nothing.
	I killed someone. You know that. That's why you're here. Why you volunteered.
Father	I'm sorry. I wanted to enjoy the show. I didn't mean to spoil it for you.
Hypnotist	Please. You didn't. Really. Since November, I –
Father	November?
Hypnotist	Since your daughter's death, I've not – I'm not. I've not been much of a hypnotist.
Father	I saw your poster for this. I recognised your name. When I saw what you did, I was interested. I thought you could help. Will you help? I need help.
	My wife – Dawn – she's very unhappy.
	I'm so sorry about this.
Hypnotist	It's fine. These things happen. It's not your fault. Here.

The **Hypnotist** *takes away the* **Father**'s *script.*

Hypnotist	Now you're clean. Look, see. Clean. The smell has gone. Has the smell gone?
	Say 'Yes'.
Father	Yes.
Hypnotist	Good. That's really good.
	Face me.
	Now I'm going to put some clothes on you. They're probably not your choice of – I mean, these are just things I've – But let's get you covered up.

The **Hypnotist** *starts to clothe the* **Father** *with imaginary clothes.*

Hypnotist   Legs in. That's it. Well done. These are good trousers, aren't they? Say 'Yes'.

Father   Yes.

Hypnotist   There was no girl you killed. No girl. Do you understand? No girl.

It was a game. I was being stupid. I was angry.

Arms out. That's it. This is a nice shirt, isn't it? It's green, isn't it? Yes? Say 'Yes'.

Father   Yes.

Hypnotist   And this pattern, it's good, isn't it? Say 'Yes'.

Father   Yes.

Hypnotist   Good. All dressed now. All better now? Yes? Say 'Yes'.

Father   Yes.

The **Hypnotist** *hands the script back to the* **Father**.

Hypnotist   We're going to go from here. From my line. 'You're all clean and put back together.'

You're all clean and put back together.

Father   Yes, I'm all put back together.

Hypnotist   Let's get you home.

Father   No.

Hypnotist   But –

Father   I wanted to see you. I wanted to talk to you at the – since the funeral. But I didn't know how to find you. I wanted to say something.

Hypnotist   Andrew.

Father   Andy.

Hypnotist   Andy.

There's really nothing I – At the inquest, I – It wasn't my fault. Your daughter was listening to music. She didn't – I –

Father   No, it's not like that. I'm not here because – I wanted to – I needed you to know. It's good news. It's good news.

Claire's fine.

Hypnotist   What do you mean?

Father   She's fine. I mean she's okay.

She's not okay.

I mean I found her –

I haven't found her.

I mean I know where she is.

I don't know where she is.

Only.

You have to help me.

I've done something.

Something impossible.

And I don't know how I did it.

Something miraculous.

But it's not good.

It's no good.

And I don't know what to do.

I don't know what to do.

Will you help me?

Bach plays.

The **Hypnotist** *gives the following instructions directly to the*
Father:

Hypnotist   *Beautiful. I'm going to feed a speech into your ears!*
And you're going to give it directly to the audience.
Take your time. Make it your own. This space is all
yours. We start when the music stops. Over to you.

Bach stops.

Scene Five

The following speech is prompted throughout by the **Hypnotist** *who*
speaks inaudibly into a microphone, but whose words are picked up
through the **Father**'s *headphones.*

Father   Ladies and gentlemen.

Dawn went to the morgue. I refused. If
anything, in those first few days, Claire had
multiplied. She had become cloned! She was
between lines, inside circles, hiding beneath
angles. She was indentations in time, physical
depressions, imperfections on surfaces. She
was the spaces beneath the chairs.

Ladies and gentlemen.

Dawn was diminished. She clung to material
evidence. To her, Claire was a hair left on a bar
of soap, some flowers taped to a lamp post. She
was the photograph above the piano. For me,
these things were no more of Claire than of
anyone else. A photograph just looked like
other photographs. Whilst I had the real thing!

Nod your head if you understand.

The house began to fill with grief. After the
inquest, the undertakers appeared. Dawn and
Marcy discussed which of Claire's toys should

go into her coffin. On the day of the funeral I went for a walk. Dawn screamed at me, but I had no one to bury.

Nod your head if you understand.

I came to the roadside. I needed a hug from my girl. I looked at a tree. A tree by the road. I touched it. And from the hollows and the spaces, I scooped up the properties of Claire and changed the physical substance of the tree into that of my daughter.

Three. Two. One.

Bach plays.

The **Hypnotist** *gives the following instructions to the* **Father** *through the ear piece:*

> *Fantastic, X. Beautiful. I'm going to come up to you and ask you if you're okay. I'll say, 'Are you okay?' When I ask you that question take your headphones out – you will not need them again – and then ask me for a drink of water. Say, 'Can I have a drink of water?'*

Bach stops.

Scene Six

Hypnotist   Are you okay?

The **Father** *takes out their earphones.*

Father   Could I have a drink of water?

Hypnotist   Of course. Of course. I'm so sorry.

I'll have to go down to the bar and get you one; I'll be no more than a minute I promise. Will you be alright on your own? Say 'Yes'.

Father   Yes.

*The **Hypnotist** exits the stage to get a glass of water for the **Father**. He is gone no more than a minute, leaving the **Father** alone on stage with the audience.*

The sound of the roadside.

A minute, during which a lorry thunders past.

The sound of the roadside stops.

*The **Hypnotist** returns with a glass of water for the **Father**. He invites the **Father** to sit on the piano stool, and gives him a new piece of script which contains the following scene.*

*The **Hypnotist** rights one of the up-turned chairs from the act and sits on it.*

Hypnotist   Okay?

Father   Yes.

Hypnotist   You're doing brilliantly.

                How are you feeling about it?

Father   Fine.

Hypnotist   Not embarrassed?

Father   A bit.

Hypnotist   You should have said, I'd have stopped.

Father   It's okay.

Hypnotist   Still nervous?

Father   A bit.

Hypnotist   It doesn't show.

                I thought I saw you struggling to keep a straight face earlier on.

Father   Yes!

Hypnotist	When was that?
	Was it around the wiping up the shit? People usually get the giggles around then.
Father	No, actually.
Hypnotist	When?
Father	When you said Ford Focus.
Hypnotist	What?
Father	I used to drive a Ford Focus.
Hypnotist	No way! How funny!
	What do you think's going to happen?
Father	I don't know.
Hypnotist	Who's your favourite character?
Father	Nobody really.
Hypnotist	Do you get the story?
Father	About the girl?
Hypnotist	I suppose so.
Father	I get that she's dead. Or is that all in his mind?
Hypnotist	Whose?
Father	Mine. The father's.
Hypnotist	No, she really is dead.
Father	And you killed her?
Hypnotist	Indirectly, yes.
Father	I don't understand the stuff with the tree, then.
Hypnotist	No.
Father	I feel sorry for his wife.
Hypnotist	Dawn?

Father   And his other daughter. The one who's watching *The Simpsons*.

Hypnotist   Marcia.

Father   How old is she meant to be?

Hypnotist   I don't know. Whatever you think.

Father   It feels like she's about five?

Hypnotist   Five's good. She's a little under-written.

Father   Yes.

Do we ever get to see her?

Hypnotist   She appears as a chair.

Father   Okay

Hypnotist   In about ten minutes time.

Father   Okay.

Could I ask a question about my character?

Hypnotist   Of course.

Father   What does he do for a living?

Hypnotist   I've always assumed he's a teacher.

Father   Okay.

Of art or something?

Hypnotist   I always assumed maths, or geography.

Father   Oh.

Hypnotist   Is it important?

Father   Not really.

Hypnotist   Are you okay if we get back to it?

Father   Of course.

Hypnotist	You're really good, you know. And you're doing really well.
Father	So are you.
	It's really well written.
Hypnotist	Thanks.
	Can I ask you to go and sit back in the audience?
Father	In the pub?
Hypnotist	Yes.
Father	But they've all gone.
Hypnotist	Yes. The show was a failure; they became embarrassed and left. It's what I'm used to. Don't worry on my behalf. For the last three months, since the accident, I've been – I've lost all ability. Like I said, honouring old bookings.
Father	I'm sorry.
Hypnotist	I've lost my mojo! Have to think about a career change. Could be worse, I could be dead!
	God, I'm sorry. I'm so sorry.
Father	It's fine. It's not really me.
Hypnotist	Of course not.
Father	And anyway, it hasn't happened yet.
Hypnotist	What?
Father	You said it's a year from now.
Hypnotist	Yes! Of course.
Father	So.
	If you'll excuse me.
Hypnotist	Of course.

Father   If we're a year in the future –

Hypnotist   Yes.

Father   – and the accident was three months ago –

Hypnotist   Go on.

Father   – then, on another level, the accident's also going to happen in nine months time. Nine months from now, here, in the theatre. Is that right?

Hypnotist   I suppose so.

Father   This sounds stupid but –

Hypnotist   Go on.

Father   Is there nothing we can do to stop it happening?

Hypnotist   I'm so sorry.

Father   You will help me, though, won't you?

Hypnotist   I don't see what else I can do.

Father   Dawn says I need closure.

Hypnotist   I'm not really a therapist.

Father   I've thought about suicide.

Hypnotist   I –

                 Three. Two. One.

Scene Seven

Music plays loud. The come-on-down music from the **Hypnotist**'s *act.*

During the music, the **Hypnotist** *provides the* **Father** *with a script and a microphone and instructs them directly on what to do.*

The **Hypnotist** *picks up another chair and places it behind the* **Father***'s piano stool, where the* **Hypnotist** *will sit, his back to the* **Father** *and the audience.*

Music stops.

Father	Dawn.
	Dawn.
Hypnotist	Sssh.
Father	Dawn.
Hypnotist	What?
Father	You still crying?
Hypnotist	I'd just got to sleep. I was sleeping.
Father	It's okay.
Hypnotist	Andy.
Father	I wanted to read something to you.
Hypnotist	You'll wake Marcy.
Father	Help you to relax. It's from one of the books – the books they left – You don't have to do anything.
Hypnotist	I can't stand this. I was asleep, Andy.
Father	Listen. It's a script. It will help you.
Hypnotist	Please.

The **Father** *will read the following speech through the microphone.*

At the same time, the **Hypnotist** *will become increasingly distraught and upset, delivering Dawn's words over the* **Father***'s speech.*

Gradually the 'hypnotic' music from the stage act starts to be heard – playing from the same place as the Bach and the roadside. This will build slowly throughout.

Father

'I want you to imagine that you are lying on a golden sandy beach. And as you lie under the warmth of the sun, I want you to feel all the muscles in your body are beginning to relax. All the tension is beginning to melt away.'

'Your heels are sinking gently into the soft, warm sand.'

'Your ankles, your calves, the backs of your knees, your thighs, your buttocks, your sacrum, the small of your back, your spine sinks down, vertebrae by vertebrae, your rib cage, your shoulders, the nape of the neck, the back of the neck, your head.'

'Sinking further and further, relaxing deeper and deeper. All tension bleeding out of your body and into the golden sands. As you breathe in and out, in and out, I want you to be receptive to the thought that you're letting go of all anxiety, fear, sadness, anger,

Hypnotist

I can't bear this.

I can't stand this, Andy, please. What's happening?

Has it not sunk in yet? Is that what's happened? Well it had better sink in soon, cos I can't do this on my own. I can't stand this. It's three o'clock in the morning, Andy, and our beautiful daughter is lying in a fridge somewhere and you're asking me to relax my fucking knees.

Don't you go mad on me, man. I need you. This is hell. If it weren't for Marcy I'd be under a car. I'd be at the bottom of a lake, off a bridge, under a train, hanging from a fucking beam. Don't you feel it? Oh god, oh god. You don't get it. Claire's

'grief or any other feeling
and emotion that is holding
you back.'

'You're breathing now in
rhythm with the waves that
are gently lapping at your
feet. The water is clear and
sparkling. It is glinting in
the dappled sunshine. As the
water plays around your
body you begin to make a
conscious connection from
your heart to the whole of
creation. And as you
breathe, you feel your body
sinking lower and lower into
the sand, at all times
supported by the earth that
is so rich, so abundant, so
unconditional that her
energies can provide you
with all you're asking for.'

gone, Andy. She's gone.

You're not even listening.
It's like some abstract
intellectual fucking
concept for you, isn't it.
Claire's death. She never
existed for you in the
first place, did she? She
was just some idea. The
idea of a daughter, just as
I'm the idea of a wife.
Marcy's the idea of a
child. We don't exist for
you, do we, not in flesh
and blood. So you
haven't lost anything,
have you. She's still
there, in your head,
where she was in the first
fucking place. Well I
have. I fucking have.
Help me.

Father   'Here begin to create the intention of
collecting the subtle qualities you require
to help you on your life's journeys, such as
balance, health, clarity, courage. Be aware
that as the waters lap around you, your body
sinks under and is redeemed of all loss, all
negativity. And when at last the waters recede,
they leave you feeling completely refreshed
and totally relaxed.'

The trance music stops.

'These are instructions for a mental exercise.
Practice each day for one hour. Use caution in

> **releasing yourself at the end of each period of exercise.'**

Bach plays. The **Hypnotist** *instructs the* **Father.**

Hypnotist   Fantastic, X! This music's going to play. I'm going to come and stand downstage. When the music stops I want you to give me that next line on your script – the line is, 'You've woken Marcy'. And then we're going to carry on with the scene.

You are doing brilliantly.

Bach stops.

Father   You've woken Marcy.

Hypnotist   I need to clear this up. Pack the car. Could I have the microphone please?

The **Father** *hands the* **Hypnotist** *the microphone.*

Hypnotist   All this stuff is mine, the speakers – I suppose I should sell it. I sold that Ford Focus.

Father   Do I stay here? Do I stay sitting?

Hypnotist   I don't know.

Father   You said I was doing brilliantly.

Hypnotist   You are.

Father   You said we could stop if I wasn't enjoying it.

Hypnotist   That was just a thing to say, to encourage you.

Father   I want to stop.

Hypnotist   Listen.

She just stepped out. That's all. I went round to the front of the car. You could still hear the music playing from her headphones.

Father   She could really play.

Hypnotist   I'm sure she could.

Father   I loved to listen to her, watch her fingers.

Hypnotist   I have to go, Andy. Or they'll kick us out.

Father   And then tonight!

I couldn't play the piano before tonight. Didn't know I could play.

I was good, wasn't I?

Hypnotist   Stand up.

Stand here.

The **Hypnotist** *positions the* **Father** *in relation to the piano stool and takes away their script.*

Hypnotist   You're cold in this rain.

Three, two, one.

The sound of the roadside cuts in.

The **Hypnotist** *is there, holding a chair on his hip, as he would a five year old girl.*

Hypnotist   Are you coming home?

Come home, it's fucking freezing.

The **Hypnotist** *may feed the* **Father** *the following instruction:*

'Don't repeat anything now, X. Just listen to what you say.'

You say, 'I can't leave'.

I say, 'She's not here'.

You say, 'You can't see'.

I say, 'Where then? Where is she?'

You say, 'Here. Here'.

I say, 'It's a tree, Andy. It's just a fucking tree'.

You say, 'No, you're wrong'.

I say, 'It's alright, Marcy. Daddy's poorly. Oh, you're frozen, you poor thing. Let's get you home'.

I say, 'Look, she's lost her sister. She's not going to lose her fucking father, too.'

I say, 'We all have to deal with this. Cope with this. We have to get on. See things for what they really are.'

Point at the piano stool.

Say, 'Look, Dawn, look'.

Father   Look, Dawn, look.

Hypnotist   Say, 'It's not a tree anymore'.

Father   It's not a tree anymore.

Hypnotist   Say, 'You're not looking'.

Father   You're not looking.

Hypnotist   Say, 'I've changed it into Claire'.

Father   I've changed it into Claire.

Hypnotist   I say, 'Our girl is dead, love. She's dead'.

I say, 'That is a tree, I am your wife, this is your daughter, that is a road. This is what matters. This. This is what we have to deal with. This.'

The sound of a lorry thundering past.

The road side noise ends abruptly.

*The **Hypnotist** gets the **Father** to sit on the piano (which was the tree) and hands them a script. The **Hypnotist** then sits on a righted chair.*

Hypnotist   Is it how you imagined it?

Father   What?

Hypnotist   Doing this.

Father   The whole coming on stage thing?

Hypnotist   Yes, the whole thing.

Father   I didn't really know what to expect.

Hypnotist   Why did you agree?

Father   It sounded interesting.

Hypnotist   Don't you think it's a bit contrived?

Father   Hard to tell from here.

Hypnotist   Of course!

                 Have you seen any of my other work?

Father   No.

                 Also –

                 Dawn says it's as though there's been two
                 deaths. She says if I don't sort my head out
                 soon she's taking Marcy.

                 So I ought to do something.

                 I think it's because I never went to the morgue.

                 If I'd been able to see her for one last time. If
                 I'd been able to say goodbye.

                 If I could just say goodbye.

                 And when I saw your name on a poster.

Hypnotist   You thought I could help with that?

Father   Say.

                 Say, 'I'm sorry'.

Hypnotist   I'm sorry.

Father	Say, 'I have to pack up'.
Hypnotist	I have to pack up.
	You know there wasn't a piano.
Father	What?
Hypnotist	Earlier. There wasn't really a piano.
Father	Yes. I played it. I played it earlier on.
Hypnotist	No! That was just me playing some music and saying that there was.
Father	No!
	I really played it!!

Scene Eight

Music plays, loud. Carmina Burana, O Fortuna.

The music stops.

The **Hypnotist** *gives a series of instructions to the* **Father***, audible to the audience.*

Hypnotist   These are the last speeches in the play. We give them directly out to the audience. Take your time. Make them your own. Feel your way. X, you've been brilliant.

Both actors read from scripts directly out to the audience. As the two actors read, the Bach begins to play, quietly.

Hypnotist   When I say so, you're driving.

It's dusk. The sky is purple, blue, orange, yellow, grey.

To your right, the rim of the world is blackening.

You're on your way to somewhere. You're not too tired.

You shift your weight. You shift your weight again.

You glance at the mirror. You catch sight of the upper left-hand corner of your face.

You're fifty-nine.

You're driving forward in space and time.

Father   When I say so, you're walking.

It's dusk.

You're on your way to somewhere. You shift your weight. You shift your weight again.

You're twelve.

The air is cold. You're listening to music. You're not too tired.

You're walking forward in space and time.

Hypnotist   When I count to three, you're cornering. You're reaching for a cigarette.

Nod your head if you understand.

Father   When I count to three you're dreaming of winter and supper and Futurama. Your cheeks are flushed with
the cold.

Nod your head if you understand.

Hypnotist   When I click my fingers, you're swerving. Your hands are gripping the steering wheel, your foot is jabbing hard on the brakes.

Father   When I click my fingers, you're stepping off the kerb.

Hypnotist	When I say sleep, a girl is there. Her eyes are wide open.
	When I say sleep, she looks at you.
	When I say sleep everything slows.
Father	When I say sleep a car is coming towards you. You're listening to music.
	When I say sleep, the music stops.
Hypnotist	When I say sleep, she lifts her hand up.
	When I say sleep, you say goodbye.
Father	When I say sleep, everything stops
Hypnotist	When I say sleep, you're free again.
Father	When I say sleep, you're free.
Hypnotist	Sleep.
Father	Sleep.
Hypnotist	When you open your eyes.
Father	When you open your eyes.

The music passes through into the First Variation, which plays forcefully through to an end.

Blackout.

End.

9 781350 437609